A Path to Inner Peace

HOW TO HAVE A WELL-BALANCED LIFE WITH GOD

Evangelist Sonya Gray

Rain Publishing
Knightdale, North Carolina

Copyright © 2014 by Sonya Gray.

All rights reserved. No part of this publication may be reproduced, distributed or transmitted in any form or by any means, including photocopying, recording, or other electronic or mechanical methods, without the prior written permission of the publisher, except in the case of brief quotations embodied in critical reviews and certain other noncommercial uses permitted by copyright law. For permission requests, write to the publisher, addressed "Attention: Permissions Coordinator," at the address below.

Sonya Gray
P.O. Box 171143
Spartanburg, SC 29301
www.srministries.org

Cover Image/Design: www.CitisonshipDesign.com
Edited by Rain Publishing, LLC.
www.RainPublishing.com

Ordering Information: Quantity sales. Special discounts are available on quantity purchases by corporations, associations, and others. For details, contact the "Special Sales Department" at the address above.

A Path to Inner Peace/ Sonya Gray. —1st ed.
ISBN 978-0-9916618-0-0
Library of Congress: 2014936243

Contents

The Triangle of Life.................................. 1

Preparation for Intimacy...................... 9

Experiencing God through Jesus 27

Passion to Know Him........................... 31

Hindrance to Intimacy with God 37

Embracing a Relationship with Self... 43

Developing Your Relationship with God 53

God Working in You 59

Dedication

To my Lord and Savior Jesus Christ who is everything to me, thank you for equipping me to write your word to help other women have a balanced life through you.

To Apostle Ron & Hope Carpenter - for your impartation into my life on the matter of peace. Because of you, I have a well-balanced life through the word of God.

To my best friends - Kimberly Hardman, Joyce Webster, and Barbara Pickens, thank you for inspiring me to stay focused on God and my purpose. It is truly a blessing to have true people of God in my life.

To Evangelist Hasker Hudgens - thanks for helping me grow and helping me reach the relationship that I desired with God and others through ministry. Thanks for helping me realize that I did not need a title to be a leader.

To my Spiritual Mother - Olivia Miller, thank you for pushing me to follow my dreams and stay focused on the thing God put in me from my mother's womb. I love you and I thank God for the healing power He worked in you. God Bless.

To Pastor Horace and Barbara Wilson, thanks for being a positive role model for me all my life.

To my husband - Roosevelt Gray Jr., thanks for putting up with me for over 20 years and standing beside me when I need to talk, vent, or just cry. You have been awesome and may God continue to bless you.

Acknowledgments

I would like to give special thanks:

To my children, Torez and Brittany Gray, you are everything to me and I am a better person because of you.

To my wonderful grandsons, Bre'land Hunter Gray and Terrance Lamar Means Jr., this one is for you and I can't wait to see what God does in you. You are my little Bishops.

To my mother - Barbara T. Anderson thanks for being who you are and giving birth to me.

To my sisters and brothers, Kim, Dwan, Ursula, Aaron (RIP), Alphaeus, Marcus, Marcel Anderson and Lammon Campbell - thanks for just being in the will of God and always putting God first.

To my amazing sister-in-law Alexius thanks for being the woman of God you are to my brother.

To my dad - Dewayne Anderson thanks for just being who you are and also always being there for me.

To my stepmother - Altie Anderson thanks for encouraging me to be who I am in my walk with God and being in my life.

To my nieces and nephews, Jessica, Karsen, Christopher, Zavion, and Elijah, keep God first and all of you will go far.

To my extended family and friends thanks for always being there and pouring into me the wisdom needed to survive. I love you.

To my spiritual daughters - Autumn Sullivan, Corinthia Harris, Felecia Wilson, Kaneshia Goldsmith, Mia Cohen, Kimberly Hudgens and Faith & Rachelle Hudgens, I thank God for allowing you to be in my life at this very important time. I love all of you. Keep God first and you will go far. Thanks for being women of excellence.

To my spiritual sons, Kristopher Dillard, Fred Giles, Christian Wilson, Walter Dyals, and Alan Goggins you are all mighty men of valor and I thank God for the example you are going to be to the next generation of young men.

To a very special young lady - Shan Shan, you have truly been blessed by God. You did not let circumstances keep you from achieving what God had planned for you. I admire you for that. Love you.

To my amazing Cousin Lucinda Hillstock who has inspired and pushed me to go further. I love you cousin and am thankful to God for all you do to push me.

To all my RWOC Movement Students, this is for you and to let you know that all things are possible with God on your side.

Lastly, Rain Publishing, what can I say, thanks for coming into my life at such a time as this. I knew the day Marcel introduced me to you it was God ordained. Rachel and Jeff Smith, God is definitely taking you higher and greater is coming.

Preface

I am thankful that God has chosen me to write this book, which has been prepared with much love and prayer. I asked God to give me the material that women need and I believe He has done just that.

We are living in a time when most believers are going through some type of trial, tribulation, sickness or some transitional discomfort. I am reminded of what Paul said in II Corinthians 3:18, "But we all with unveiled face, beholding as in a mirror the glory of the Lord, are being transformed into the same image from glory to glory, just as by the Spirit of the Lord." We are growing from glory to glory in the Lord. I believe the greater the level of growth, the greater the trial. I can testify to that. Often in these times of testing and trials, we experience a season of drought, a time when we cannot hear the voice of the Lord directing us. It is at this time we have to walk by faith. I was once told that when you're taking a test the teacher rarely talks except to give instructions. I think that is true with God. He has already taught us what we need to know to go through this season and all we have to do is walk it out by faith. In most cases we are like babes, we want to stay on milk and God is showing us through the trial that it is well time to be on the meat of the Word of God. Remember, your trials are only final exams that you have to pass to go to the next level of Glory that the heavenly Father has for you.

I truly pray that this book will bless your life and in the days to come when you're up against the wall, you will pull out this book, meditate on the scriptures, put on your fighting garment and continue to stand. Paul says, "When you have done all you can do keep standing." Making it through life's challenges is not as hard when you have balanced your life by developing a relationship with God, yourself and your neighbor. I have put much time and prayer on the subject of developing a relationship with God because I believe that a relationship with God is the key to a balanced life, including education, singleness, marriage or whatever comes your way. Your relationship with God first, yourself, and then others is the path to inner peace.

To God Be the Glory,

Evangelist Sonya Gray

A Well Balanced Life consists of:
Relationship with God
Relationship with Self
Relationship with Others

CHAPTER ONE

The Triangle of Life

Matthew 22:36-39
Deuteronomy 6:4-5, 10: 12-13

There are three areas in a woman's life that must come into complete harmony in order for her to experience Inner Peace. In this book we will discuss these three areas as the "Triangle of Life." First, the foundation of developing a relationship with and loving God, secondly, developing a relationship with and loving yourself and then developing a relationship with and loving others. These things are not possible without developing an intimate relationship with God.

A woman's way of life should lead her to a place of completion and peace. Our lives should be like a well-constructed group of musical notes that make a sweet song. There should be internal peace, tranquility, and a systematic arrangement of relationships that bring one to completion. One must have a peace that brings completion and wholeness, lacking nothing, which will make beautiful music unto God.

What is the meaning of balance? Balance means: stability by even distribution of weight in each area of peace. One who has good spiritual equilibrium has a state of spiritual balance: Spirit, Soul and Body, which is a state of balance of opposing factors. We are a Spirit with a soul living in a body; the opposing forces are the Spirit and the Soul. Paul says in Romans 7:14-25, "There are two laws operating, the law of Spirit and Life and the law of Sin and Death. I don't know what is happening in my body, the thing I will to do I don't do and the things I don't want to do I find myself doing. O wretched man that I am, who shall deliver me from this death, with the Spirit I serve God, with the mind I serve the law of God and with the body the law of sin and death." The body cannot be saved but the Spirit of the Living God can control it.

Balance brings on peace. Imagine a well- tuned choir. When a choir is practicing it sounds ugly and confusing but when the director gets everyone organized it sounds like beautiful music. This is balance.

Who can function when there is a lot of noise, the children fighting, the baby crying, the dishwasher is broken, the washing machine is running over, there is trouble on the job, or your marriage is in trouble? Noise is coming from all directions, what do you do? There must be balance in order to experience the peace of God in our lives. The Holy Spirit is our director and there are times in our lives that He waves his hand in the air during our confusion and trouble and lets us know that it is time to become balanced and sing a beautiful song for God.

There must be balance in the life of every believer. Too much of anything can bring imbalance, such as too much Word and no faith. The Word has to be properly disseminated, if not you will become obese with the Word of God and have no works. When a sheep has eaten too much and needs to be sheered, he falls over, cannot get himself up and he dies in that state. There must be balance in our lives to have inner peace.

You are out of balance when: you want to preach and don't want to pray, when you want to speak for God and you don't want to speak to God, when you want your lover more than you want God, when physical bread is more important to you than the Bread of Life, and when you should be at the feet of Jesus and you're at the stove cooking or being troubled by so many things. Sometimes you can even be doing a good thing at the wrong time.

Being balanced means being in the right place, at the right time. In Luke 10:38 we see two sisters: Mary and Martha, one out of balance and one balanced.

Jesus was at Bethany on His way to the cross and He needed this time to be in a quiet place and minister to those whom He loved. Jesus never said He wanted to eat and that's where

Martha was out of balance. She never sought God to see what He desired of her. There is nothing wrong with cooking and serving but it is not what was needed at that hour. Martha was busy doing a good thing at the wrong time. Mary was very balanced, all she wanted to do was sit in the presence of the Lord at His feet. Whenever you read about Mary, you will find her in this humble position at the feet of Jesus. In Luke 10:39, Mary sat at the feet of Jesus listening to Him talk; in John 11:32, she fell at His feet when He came to raise Lazarus from the dead and in John 12:1-3, Mary anointed Jesus' feet with a very costly oil before He went to the cross. A place of balance is a place of humility and sensitivity to the spirit of the Living God, a place where you are at peace inside yourself and in the world. No matter the trial, the trouble or sickness, you can find peace in God's Word and in His presence.

The first part of the triangle of life is the foundation. Everything that you build must have a good foundation. The height of a building depends on the depth of the foundation, the deeper a foundation, the taller a building can be built on it. The building is only as strong as the foundation you build it on. The weaker and the shallower the foundation a woman builds on, the weaker and the shallower the woman becomes. A shallow woman cannot stand for, against, or through anything.

While developing relationships the way gets hard, rocky, and stormy but if you have built a solid relationship with God, your life is like a palm tree. You may rock back and forth, you might bend but you will not be blown down. You might break but your roots will stay secure in the foundation. You rarely see a skyscraper blown over by a storm because the foundation is secure. God is the foundation that we should build on; you have to get to know Him.

God wants intimacy with us, He is calling for us, He is visiting us in our dreams, in our spirits and even in the trouble we are experiencing. He wants us to spend time with Him and get to know Him.

CHAPTER TWO

Preparation for Intimacy

"That I May Know Him..."
Philippians 3:10

God wants to have fellowship with the believer but we first have to get to know Him, experience Him and who He desires to be in our lives. All He wants is for us to love Him, trust Him, obey Him and serve Him. The relationship begins with Love. God is love and everything He does is based upon His Agape love. Paul said Christ loved us so much that "while I was still a sinner

He died for me." His love would not wait until I made up my mind to accept Him, because I didn't have the power to do it myself. I couldn't be saved apart from the death, burial, and resurrection of Jesus Christ. It is through His love and His blood that I am saved and filled with the Holy Spirit.

In Deuteronomy 6, we find a celebration that is called the "Shema." The Shema is 'the basic Jewish confession of faith.' "Hear Oh Israel: The Lord our God is one Lord: And thou shall love the Lord thy God with all thine heart, and with all thy soul, and with all thy might. And these words, which I command thee this day, shall be in thine heart" (Deut. 6:4-6). This passage depicts total self-surrender of the whole being to God. True love, true worship, and true holy principles come from the heart, as do the evil issues of life. When we love God with all that is within us, there is little room in our heart for anything else but love.

One reason we have such a difficult time developing a relationship with God is because we wait until we get older or when we are going through a trial and already set in our beliefs. Moses said that God's Word should be taught and meditated on, "Thou shalt teach them diligently unto thy children and shalt talk of them when thou sittest in thine house, and when thou walkest by the way and when thou liest down and when thou risest up" (Deuteronomy 6:7). If we start teaching our children the love of God when they are very young, perhaps they will not have difficulties in developing a personal relationship with God when they are older.

In Deuteronomy 6:4, the word "hear," in Hebrew is again the word

"Shema." This verse starts with a command for the people to love God and respond to Him properly. It clearly gives a reason for developing a relationship with God and is a command that we are to "love the Lord with all our Heart, Soul and Body." In this text the covenant name for God is Jehovah Elohim. The word Elohim is 'plural God'. Though He is plural, God is yet one God; He is God the Father, God the Son and God the Holy Spirit. Man is a spirit, with a soul and lives in a body. The Tabernacle is one building with three sections: the outer court, the inner court and the Holy of Holies.

It is suggested that the word love here means to make a choice to accept God and obey Him. King Josiah is a perfect example of that love. King Josiah loved God and he obeyed His law to the letter. There was no other King who obeyed the law and trusted God as he did. His grandfather Hezekiah too was famed for his love, trust and obedience to God.

God loves us and He wants us to love Him as well. The scriptures declare that God desires a relationship with His creation. God desires that the believer love Him with all that is within themselves. God is a jealous God; His commandment states that we are to have no other God before Him.

Let's take a look back into time and see where we have come from to bring us to this awesome point in our lives, an opportunity to get to know Him and experience God Almighty. One would need to take a look at the practices of old, to take a close look at the religious practice of worship and the method used to make atonement for sin. The old covenant did not wash away sin, it covered sin. The order of worship was not designed for the believer to develop a relationship with God nor the opportunity to fellowship with Him. When the children of Israel left Egyptian bondage, they left depending on Moses' faith and relationship with God. As a result, whenever trouble came, such as a lack of food or a lack of water they complained, cried, and wanted to go back into slavery. That is so much like believers today. When we fall into a little turbulence, we are ready to give up and turn back to the old unhappy situations we were in rather than use the experience to get to know God and trust Him to bring us out on top.

For the Old Testament Israelites, there was little opportunity to develop a relationship with God because they always saw God through the eyes of Moses. God always made His presence known before the children of Israel to assure them that "He would never leave them and He would never forsake them." Although they could never see Him or talk to Him directly, they saw Him in a cloud, a pillar of fire or smoke but when Jesus arrived they were able to touch Him, talk to Him and see miracles performed through Him. Under the old covenant, it was like God walked in the shadow of Himself. If God could experience loneliness or pain, what a lonely, painful life He would have lived, only appearing on the backside of the mountain in a private meeting with Moses. He was like an 18th century monster that had to creep around, hiding from the people He loved. It is like the Hunchback of Notre Dame, a misfit who was so misunderstood that he crept around in the dark. The truth of the matter is that if His glory had been seen directly by the people, they would have been consumed and died. God told Moses "I can only let you see my backside."

Everything in the Old Testament was a symbol, a foreshadowing of things to come, the coming of the Lord

Jesus Christ. The purpose of building the Tabernacle was to make a place for God to dwell among the people. God desires to dwell with His redeemed people; He dwelled with Adam and Eve in the Garden before the fall. He walked and talked with Abraham, Noah, Moses, David, Solomon and the Prophets. He created the Tabernacle for a place of fellowship. He made His Word flesh to "dwell" among us and now He dwells inside each redeemed believer, (II Corinthians 6:19). The Tabernacle was a place where the Spirit of God would reside and the priest would make sacrificial offerings for the people.

At the beginning of the 25th chapter of Exodus, God gave Moses instructions on the building of the Tabernacles. God asked the people for specific gifts that were given freely and not under compulsion. The people gave such items that were requested to show their desire to worship Him. God did not need the gifts for Himself but He received them because it represented their love and worship for Him.

All of the stations in the Tabernacle were a foreshadowing of Jesus. There were three sections of the Tabernacle:

I. The Outer Court-Representing the Body.
   1. The Brazen Altar was the area where the people brought their lambs for sacrifice. The lamb's life was sacrificed for the sins of the owner. The owner would lay his hand over the head of the lamb, and then the lamb was killed. This process was a type of cleansing of sins, through the covering of the blood of the lamb. In Hebrews 10:4, Paul states, "It is

not possible that the blood of bulls and goats could take away sins." Verses 8-9 read, "Sacrifice and offering, burnt offerings, and offerings for sin you did not desire, nor had pleasure in them." Jesus came to do the will of God and took away the first covenant so that He may establish the second. We have been sanctified through the offering of the body of Jesus Christ once for all. Jesus took care of the need for making sacrifices. Paul, the author of Hebrews gives a contrast between Jesus' death and the sacrificial lambs. Hebrews 10:11-12 shows that there were always sins to be atoned and sacrifices being made. Jesus offered Himself as a sacrifice and then sat down at the right hand of His Father. Sitting down was an indication that His work for redemption was finished. Now when the believer sins, I John 1:9 states, "If we confess our sins, He is faithful and just to forgive us our sins and to cleanse us from all unrighteousness."

II. The Inner Court-Represents the Soul of Man
   1. The Lampstand- The Lampstand has seven cups. The number seven represents God's completion; the Lampstand was a foreshadowing of Jesus being the Light of the World. The oil represented the Holy Spirit who has anointed us. Today each believer represents the light of the Holy Spirit because they're now

the Temple of the true and living God.

2. The Table of Shewbread - The Shewbread Table was placed on the north side of the Tabernacle. The twelve loaves of bread represented the twelve tribes of Israel. They are a type of Christ who is the Bread of Life.

3. There was a Veil that separated the Holy Place from the Most Holy Place. The Veil was of a linen fabric, brilliantly colored in blue, purple and scarlet. When Jesus gave up the ghost on the cross, the veil was torn, which enabled the believer to go into the Most Holy Place. Jesus is our Great High Priest and we are invited by Him to come into

the most Holy place "to obtain mercy and grace in a time of trouble." (Hebrews 4:14-16, Matthew 27:51).

III. The Holy of Holies-The Most Holy Place-Represents the Spirit
1. The Ark of the Covenant - it was here that the very Shekinah Glory of God resided. In the Tabernacle the Most Holy Place was God's throne room where His glory resides. The contrast is that now God dwells in the heart of the believer, which Paul stated in I Corinthians 6:19, "Do you not know that your body is the Temple of the Holy Ghost?" Under the old covenant, only the High Priest was permitted to go into the area of the Ark of the Covenant. Because of the cross, the believer is invited to come in

boldly and obtain mercy and grace in a time of trouble. Jesus is now our Great High Priest.

Matthew 22:37 states that we are to love the Lord God with all of our heart, soul and body, the same as in the Old Testament. We were created to fellowship with God. He sent His Son from heaven to earth to show us the real essence of Himself. John 1:18 states that "No one has ever seen God, but God the Son, who is at the Father's side." Jesus came into this world not only to die and save us but He came to make God known on earth. Only the essence of God's majestic glory was seen in the Old Testament. While it is stated in Exodus that "no man can see God's face and live," it is also recorded that Jacob while wrestling with the angel saw God, and that Abraham (called friend of God) and Moses had also seen God. The Israelites were able to witness the essence of His glory in a tangible way. As they journeyed to the Promised Land, they experienced God's glory by the pillar of fire that guided them by night and the pillar of cloud that guided them by day. When Moses went to the Tabernacle, the glory cloud would hover over the Tabernacle, when Moses went up the mountain, he would experience the glory of God. What an advantage we have today in developing a relationship with God. The very spirit of God abides within the believer.

Often we see God in the light of what He has done for us and not who He really is, simply because we have not developed a relationship with Him. Many of us don't really want God but we want His goods, we want what He has to offer us. We try to step into His presence only when we need Him. We call out to Him when we need Him to pay a light bill, to pay the house note, to make our enemies leave us alone or to bring a husband back home.

No saints, God wants you. He doesn't need you but He loves you and He wants you. God wants us to draw near to Him and He surely will draw near to us. In Isaiah 54:5, we find where God is encouraging Jerusalem and telling them that they will reproduce again, they will no longer be barren. He says, "Your creator is your husband and the God of Hosts is His name." In this passage of scripture He is depicted as a provider, protector and a fierce and mighty warrior crushing His enemies in battle. We only look to God to provide for us and protect us but God wants to do so much more in our lives. To experience Him in that way will require developing a relationship and intimacy with Him.

The body of Christ is just like Israel; we go after other gods (idols), whether they're members of our families, our homes, cars or jobs. Anything that keeps you away from a first priority devotion to God is considered a god. Over and over God calls His wayward, adulterous, and idolatrous wife Israel to come back to Him to love Him. God said to Israel, after she had done all these things, "Return to me," but Israel did not return."

David is one of the Old Testament figures who knew how to love God and have a strong relationship with Him. He was considered the 'apple of God's eye.' Society has taught man that men who love men are weak. Lest we think that loving God with affection and intensity is not masculine, let us consider this great man. David was a mighty warrior and a fearless ruler who subdued the land and then united the kingdom, courageous to kill a lion, a bear and a giant. He was loyal to Saul and a faithful friend to Jonathan. David was an anointed musician and a songwriter. He even danced before the Lord with complete abandonment of who he was. More than all of this, David loved God! David trusted God. David obeyed God and when he fell into sin, he quickly repented as he cried out to God, "have mercy upon me, O God, according to thy loving-kindness: according unto the multitude of thy tender mercies, blot out my transgressions. Wash me thoroughly from mine iniquity, and cleanse me from my sin" (Psalm 51: 1-2).

David's love is expressed in the Psalms, such as Psalms 18:1, 31:23, 42, 68 and 116:1. It was perhaps David's love for God that inspired his son Solomon to write the Song of Solomon.

Through passionately seeking God daily, reading His word, fasting and praying you can and will have a more intimate relationship with God.

CHAPTER THREE

Experiencing God through Jesus

In the New Testament we find Jesus Christ, the embodiment of God carrying on the work of His Father. Jesus is love incarnate; He came to exemplify the love of His Father. John 3:16 states, "For God so loved the world that He gave His only begotten Son that whoever believes in Him should not perish but have everlasting life."

Jesus knows God like no other. Saint John declares that "In the beginning was the Word and the Word was with God and the Word was God, He was with God in the beginning. Through Him all things were made; without Him nothing was made that has been made" (John 1). Jesus is the Eternal Word of God. He has no beginning and He has no end, He is Alpha and Omega the beginning and the end. Jesus was always with God, when He created the heavens and the earth. He is the Creative Word of God.

"Jesus the Word became flesh and made His dwelling among us. We have seen His glory, the glory of the One and only, who came from the Father, full of grace and truth."
John 1:14

Jesus transitioned Himself from heaven to earth for the creation of God. He went through kenosis, the process of divesting Himself of His glory, putting on an earth suit and dwelling with man on earth.

It is difficult for little babes in the world to experience God because babies have to see it, touch it and smell it to believe it. The Bible says that it is impossible to please God without faith. We must have faith in Him and His existence to be saved, and to be blessed. God so loved the world that He sent His Son Jesus as an example of His love and desire to fellowship with His creation. Through the love of Jesus, as He walked on earth, we were able to actually touch God and experience the real effect of His love without being consumed and dying.

John 14:7-11 says, "If ye had known me, ye should have known my Father also: and from henceforth ye know Him and have seen Him." You cannot be passionate about someone you do not know, so you have to read and study the scriptures that will unveil

Him and give you an intimate picture of who He is. Spend time with Him in prayer and in praising and worshipping Him. Your passion for God must be greater than anything you have ever desired and you must be willing to lay aside anything that you count dear. God is a jealous God and He commands that we should have no other God but Him. God will not share His glory with anyone.

CHAPTER FOUR

Passion to Know Him

To know God not only entails knowledge of Him but also experiencing Him. Many great men have had strong relationships with God and great sacrifices were asked of them but they received great blessings as a result. Abraham was called the friend of God. He was willing to obey God and follow Him to an unknown place. He had to follow God closely and obey every Word that God spoke in order to not get lost. On another level of growth,

Abraham had to trust God in his old age to give him a son. A greater level of faith in God developed because he was far beyond childbearing age. Not only was he unable to produce, but his wife had gone through the change of life and no longer could get pregnant. This was truly a test of faith, not in what Abraham had heard about God but what he knew himself, from his personal experience with God. The next level of knowing God involved an experience of sacrificial death. God requested that Abraham offer up as a sacrifice his only son that he had been given in his old age. Abraham's willingness to obey God resulted in a relationship so strong that he was known as a friend of God.

To know God and develop a relationship with Him you have to be able to appreciate the opportunity, the invitation and the desire of God to have a relationship with the believer. Look at the extent He went to just for us to be accepted into the beloved, to walk with Him and be filled with His precious Holy Spirit.

In order to walk with God, I understand that I have to submit my body and renew my mind daily. In those areas I sometimes find myself conforming to my peers and other Christians. I must deal with the pride I have in my heritage, you know those generational curses that keep us bound by circumstances? My accomplishments were bought with blood, sweat, and tears. It was not easy to let go of the sins of this world, but I had to let it go to get to that intimate place with God. Without an intimate relationship with God it would cause me to feel self-righteous. I had to pay the price to get past that. I can walk away from them and walk into the presence of God in order to be like Him. Jesus went through too much; He divested Himself of all His glory to walk this earth to get me to the place He wants me to be. Therefore, I must divest myself of all the mess that will keep me from getting to know Him. I must empty myself; I must be delivered from that bad character.

Our lives are influenced by what we believe and whom we associate with. Paul says, "Evil company corrupts good habits" (II Corinthians 15:33). You and your associates need to be dead to the flesh (sinful nature) or in the process of dying if you are real about getting to know God. There should be no more "I," but "Christ." My ego and my pride are no longer central. I don't have to try to say the right words when I pray or talk. I don't have to try to touch God. All I have to do is be a 'dead woman' filled with God.

There are times when we just won't die and God will send us through the process of dying, shaking and burning everything that is not of Him (Hebrews 12:26-27). We go through the process of dying to self to get in position to know Him. Now I am ready to come before God as a bride does her groom. Cleansed and dressed in the right attire, I am ready for a life of intimacy with God.

Intimate relationship with God is often compared to intimacy in a marriage. How do I become intimate with God? In the same way one becomes intimate in their marriage. You take a bath, put on your makeup, comb your hair and put on your very special gown for the night.

You're not all full of food but you are full of love and expectancy for the evening of lovemaking, a time of long waited intimacy. On my wedding night my husband and I both took separate baths and brushed our teeth. I combed my hair, put on some perfume and set the atmosphere for the evening. To have a relationship with God you must keep it alive by spending time, talking, and enjoying His presence. We also must listen to Him and rarely do you want to talk.

The word intimacy simply means "to enter into me." *Enter me Lord.* When Adam knew Eve she conceived. Therefore

Adam knew Eve, and he entered her intimately. *That I may know Him.* Oh that I may be intimate with Him. Oh that He may enter me. When Jesus enters, everything changes. Isn't that what happens on your wedding night? Everything changed. Your eyes were opened to a new way of life, new feelings of fulfillment, a new level of ecstasy and you became closer to your mate.

Scripture references: I Thessalonians 4:3-5, Colossians 3:5.

CHAPTER FIVE

Hindrance to Intimacy with God

Intimacy with God has been compared to intimacy with your mate. It means you want to know Him at the deepest level. You want to be fully known and accepted for who you are. Intimacy with God means a full, fresh, moment by moment dependency upon His grace and mercy and it grows deeper with time. Always remember that it is through life's storms that you get to know God better. Spend time with Him and your life will never be the same.

Many times the development of intimacy in a marriage is difficult and in some instances is not developed. One reason is because of negative or broken emotions from past relationships or never having a good relationship with a strong father figure. Because of the vulnerability involved in intimacy, it can bring back painful experiences and memories of physical, emotional or sexual abuse. Just as those unresolved experiences could hinder a marital relationship, so can they also hinder your relationship with God. When drawing into a time of intimacy with God, one's relationship with his or her earthly father comes into play. Negative relationships and negative experiences hinder trust in God.

Without discovering the triangle of life, you will not have peace in your life. The word peace means wholeness, completion, lacking nothing. With a true relationship with God there will be no hindrance in your life - nothing missing, nothing broken. To be in peace our lives must have order. Our lives must be prioritized and we must be submitted to God. Having order is like organizing your life in such a way that you're able to meet life's demands without falling apart.

In Matthew 22:36-39, God gives us the basis for the triangle of a balanced life so we could function correctly. We must accept God's unconditional love, love ourselves, and then we are able to love others as we love ourselves.

God wants intimacy with us, He is calling for us, He is visiting us in our dreams, in our spirits, and even in the trouble we are experiencing. He wants us to spend time with Him and get to know Him. Intimacy with God is private; it's between two people, just you and God.

This intimacy is necessary in order to find peace, balance, and wholeness (Deuteronomy 10:12-13). To achieve this relationship with God we must have an intense passion and desire that saturates every aspect of life and compels us to pursue Him. Passion for God is an attitude toward the Lord Jesus Christ that begins with salvation and hopefully strengthens throughout life. As believers, we can become spiritually complacent, however content in the knowledge that we are going to heaven. If we allow religious comfort to rule our thinking, then we miss the whole point of this Christian journey. Jesus saved us so that He could live in us and through us to impact the world and other people.

We also develop a relationship with God by going into His presence just like in Psalm 63:1-11. God is the foundation. He gives us the love principle to govern our relationships. Deuteronomy 6:4-5 says, "Hear, O Israel: The Lord our God is one

Lord: and thou shalt love the Lord thy God with all thine heart and with all thy soul, and with all thy might." In John 17:21, it was the prayer of Jesus that we would be one as He and the Father are one and that we also be one in them. This requires a total self-surrender of the whole being to God.

Matthew 22:37 says, "Thou shalt love the Lord thy God with all thy heart, and with all thy soul, and with thy entire mind." To begin the process of loving God we must put away old things and put on a new body. 2 Corinthians 5:17 says, "If any man be in Christ He is a new creation, old things are passed away and behold all things become new." One must have a new heart to love God and put Him first in life and conduct. The true process of loving God is putting away flesh and opening your spirit to the gospel, taking away all hindrance in obeying the truth. Opening your heart to God by removing all reservations, covering, secrets, and unbelief, is a command and God promises to help you in this matter.

In Jeremiah 32:39 it says, "I will give them one heart, and one way, that they may fear me forever, for the good of them and of their children after them." Jesus wants to make an everlasting covenant with us that will not go away from us.

CHAPTER SIX

Embracing a Relationship with Self

God is the foundation for all relationships. Jesus is the stone-He is the rock that the builder rejected. He's the cornerstone that holds all things together. We are the living stones; we are being built up into a spiritual house, a holy priesthood, to offer up spiritual sacrifices. Acceptable to God through Jesus, we are the Temple of the Living God; the very essence and presence of God abides in us. The power that raised Jesus from the dead abides in all believers. Ephesians 3:20 says He is able "to do exceedingly abundantly above anything we could ask or think according to the power that worketh in us." You've got the power in you to BE, whomever and whatever you desire in your heart. Who you are and what you desire to be is in you, it does not matter what others might say about you or who they say you are. The power to make necessary changes in your life is in you right now. You have the power to BE according to the power of God that is working in you. Your worth is not determined by your heritage, culture, family or your environment; it is determined by the power of God that is in you.

In case you don't know who you are, you are "an heir of God and joint heir with Jesus" (Roman 8:17). We are a chosen generation, a royal priesthood, a holy nation, and His special people. We must proclaim the praises of Him who called us out of darkness into the marvelous light. We once were not God's people but are now the people of God, who had not obtained mercy but now have obtained mercy. (I Peter 2:9-10) God's love for His daughters is pure, His love for us is so pure that we will find no other like it. It is not predicated upon our performance or our appearance or our intellectual capacity. His love is the foundation that our character is built upon and all other relationships are determined by His love. If you never learn to love yourself, your entire life will be imbalanced. In accepting the LOVE of God, we will be able to accept our own inabilities and be all that we can be with what God has given to us without feeling bad about ourselves.

Sometimes it is difficult to love yourself due to childhood experiences, family relationships or adolescent challenges. If a woman doesn't have a solid relationship with herself, she will recklessly pursue external relationships in the hopes of achieving internal peace, gratification, and validation. She will try to love others in a desperate need to find in them what she must find within herself. I know this because I tried it and it did not work. This pursuit will be futile and is the cancer that kills most marriages. She will do right things for the wrong reasons, expecting someone to give her what she must give herself. She will not be able to have healthy relationships with others, because she is demanding from them what should be coming from within her. If she is married, her husband will feel guilty over his inability to satisfy what is her insatiable need. He could become reclusive and hide in the cave of his work or his recreational games, and sadly might find himself led to infidelity, since the expectations of his other woman can be controlled by the excuse of him being married.

A woman who does not love herself becomes so thirsty for love that she rushes into love half-dressed and ill-prepared. She will always love too quickly, hold on too tightly, and more often lose too quickly. If a lady relates well with herself and has strong self-esteem, she can easily share her life with another person. She sets goals and accomplishes them.

Ladies look into the mirror, see your flaws, see the bulges, and see all the imperfections. Just remember God does not see our mistakes and we must let them go and give them to Him. Can you celebrate yourself?

Whether or not you're able to celebrate what you see will determine what you expect to get out of your relationship with others. If you like what you see-celebrate it. If you don't like what you see, love yourself enough to do something about it. If you don't like it and it is painful and you have vivid remembrance of how you got it or it makes you dislike yourself, you are more than likely famished for love and will settle for anything that will give you what you should be able to give yourself. You can't expect others to do for you what you are not willing to do for yourself. Love self and then you can love others. When you have good self- esteem, you don't have to accept the opinions of others to feel good about yourself. You should reach inward before you reach outward. The way you esteem yourself will determine the kind of relationships you will have with others and your own mate. People don't like it when others try to make them over into who they want them to be. In learning to love and appreciate yourself, you can appreciate the beautiful creation God has made others to be. Matthew 22:36-39 says, "Thou shall love thy neighbor as thyself." Your love for yourself will determine what you will need to draw from other relationships in your life. A woman who loves herself is free to allow other people to be themselves. If you're a "needy person" you will ZAP all the life out of your relationships. A man flees from contention but draws strength from the woman who encourages him and affirms him. A woman who knows what to say in any given instance is a mighty powerful force. She knows how to influence her mate in positive directions.

A woman who knows and loves herself can strengthen her mate, give him courage and motivate him to be all that he can be in the Lord. Men react to praise as God reacts to praise. Praise will cause him to move to your beckoning call and to supply your every need. It is the power of the spoken word that moves men. Your words can make or break your relationship. Softness and sweetness can change the mind of a man. Always show him appreciation for the little things he does around the house, the provisions he makes for the family and the gifts he gives you no matter how small or insignificant they might seem. Keep your tongue behind the bars of your teeth. It is quick, small and deadly. Remember there is power in spoken words. Words have life and are able to produce what you say. Remember you can't always say what you think.

Ladies who love their God, love themselves and can make their husbands feel safe enough to love them and trust them.

Allow him to love a woman who is balanced, loves her God, loves herself, loves her husband and loves her neighbors as herself. Key points to remember daughter of the King, are that you cannot lead effectively if you don't know who you are and whose you are. Your perception of yourself cannot be attached to someone else. You cannot lead if you don't know your purpose or your destiny. You can't lead without a relationship with God. You can't lead where you're not willing to follow. You can't allow your spouse's status to validate you. What would happen if you lost it all? Your significance is not in externals. Externals pass away daily but the inward man is renewed day by day. Keep God at the helm of your ship and you will never sink.

CHAPTER SEVEN

Developing Your Relationship with God

Keep in mind that there are many ways in which to spend time with God. The most important thing is to begin today and spend time communicating (or talking) with God. Keep in mind that relationships take time and much attention.

Steps to Intimacy with God:

1. Decide on a place to meet God, and as much as possible consecrate that place to God.
2. Decide on a time each day to meet God. I personally believe that the time that is selected should be a sacrifice and it should be early before you begin your work day. Always know that the more time you spend with Him the greater your relationship with God becomes.
3. Decide how you will spend time with God. Make a list of activities you can do with God during your quiet time with Him. Just as you do with the one you love, make

this time exciting and interesting. Do different things to keep this time warm and intimate. In each of your visits with God seek forgiveness for all sins you have committed. Open with singing to Him, and/or playing praise music. Sing in your spirit daily. Spend time reading the Word, spend time meditating on the Word, and spend time daily worshipping God for who He is. After all of that, spend some quiet time before God, spend time just thanking God and not asking Him for anything. Lastly, pray the scriptures to Him.

Intimacy with God develops like intimacy in marriage. It's exciting at first, but takes some time to deepen.

As you move through these steps with God-Appointment, Relationship, and Trust, you will be rewarded with a deep, profound sense of intimacy with Him. You will find that you increase in knowing God, loving God, trusting God, obeying God, and serving God. Let's take a closer look at how to build or renew intimacy by pursuing these characteristics:

- **Knowing God-** The more you know God, the more you love Him, that's relationship.
- **Loving God** The more you love Him, the more you will obey Him.
- **Trusting God-**You can come to a level of trust that even when you see no way out of a storm, you know from experience you can depend upon God (Philippians 1:6).

- **Obeying God**-If you love Him, you will obey what He commands (John 14:15).
- **Serving God** - Intimacy with God causes your heart to cry out for an opportunity to express its appreciation in service. What is better than serving the one you love? Keep this in mind: True leadership is servant-hood and the greatest leader of all times was Jesus Christ. Servant-hood is an attitude exemplified by Jesus Christ, in service to others (Philippians 2:6-7).

CHAPTER EIGHT

God Working in You

In order for us to go to another level, we must first be willing to let God do a work in us. We must have a true relationship with God first and foremost. Second, we must have developed a relationship with ourselves. Lastly we must be able to get along with others in every area of ministry. My life has been a blessing from God.

In the past, I always looked to others for approval until I realized I only needed God's approval. As Romans 3:23 says, "We have all sinned, and come short of the glory of God." We can't choose what families we are born into or what happens to us in life. God knew from the foundation of the world what was going to happen to me. I now realize and appreciate my life and what trials and tribulations God has allowed me to go through. The scriptures say in James 1:3, "that the trying of your faith worketh patience." We must all have patience in every stage of life to go to the next level. We must have joy in our trials and tribulations. The scriptures say in Romans 5:3-6, that "we glory in tribulation also, knowing that tribulation worked patience. And patience; experience; and experience; hope: And hope maketh not ashamed; because the love of God is shed abroad in our heart by the Holy Ghost which is given unto us. When we were yet without strength in due time Christ died for the ungodly." Just knowing that has made my outlook on my life and others totally different. We must look to God for our every breath. He is the answer to our every need. If we lack in any area of our life it is because we have not truly applied the word of God to that area. The word of God is full of promises for us. It is time we start living like we are in heaven. We can't wait until we get to heaven to get our stuff. We must possess it now. Are we truly putting scripture to work in our lives today? I asked myself that question. I am going to get my commanded blessing from God. I am going to take ownership of everything God has promised me and then some. We must be willing to obey the word of God.

Start walking in your blessings women of God. Speak of things the way they should be. Women of God, commit and dedicate your every breath to God, so no devil in hell can invade anything in your life. I truly am a walking testimony of what God is doing and will continue to do in the life of every woman.

Notes

ABOUT THE AUTHOR

Evangelist Sonya Gray was born and raised in Spartanburg, SC. She is the oldest of nine siblings and the daughter of Dewayne Anderson and Barbara Anderson. Evangelist Gray is married to Roosevelt Gray, has two wonderful children, Torez and Brittany Williams-Gray and two precious grandsons, Bre'land Hunter Gray and Terrance Lamar Means, Jr.

Evangelist Gray has been educating and equipping youth for over 20 years. She was trained from birth to teach young men and women that God is the one who can give you inner peace. She has been through many trials and tribulations but with God on her side she has overcome every battle.

At an early age the enemy tried to kill her with drugs, alcoholism, and abusive men, however Evangelist Gray did not let these things kill her and she is still on the battle field for the Lord daily making sure no one is left behind. She knows that God is the only one who got her through all of the difficulty in her life. She had to obtain inner peace to be who she is today, a mouthpiece for the Kingdom of God and a true warrior for youth and women. She has a great passion for working with at-risk youth and is currently in the process of opening a youth and family services center for hurting families. She presently has a ministry for girls and young women between the ages of 12-19 called God's Girls Rule the World Mentoring Program. (Romans 4:17)

Evangelist Sonya Gray can be reached at her email address: srministries924@yahoo.com or mailing address P.O. Box 171143, Spartanburg, SC 29301 for speaking engagements and book signings.

May God richly bless each of you for your support.

Book Order Form

To order copies of this book, *Path to Inner Peace*, indicate the number of copies you would like next to the title, provide your shipping address and contact information, enclose payment including shipping, and mail this form to:

Evangelist Sonya Gray
P.O. Box 171143
Spartanburg, SC 29301

Path to Inner Peace @$9.99 each x____

    Shipping and Handling: $5.00
        Total Enclosed: _____

Ship to Name:

_____

Street: _____
City, State Zip

_____

Phone | Email

_____

www.ingramcontent.com/pod-product-compliance
Lightning Source LLC
Chambersburg PA
CBHW072103290426
44110CB00014B/1811